FOUNDATIONS OF OUR NATION

WRITING THE DECLARATION OF INDEPENDENCE

by Wil Mara

FOCUS READERS

FOCUS READERS

WWW.FOCUSREADERS.COM

Focus Readers is distributed by North Star Editions:
sales@northstareditions.com | 888-417-0195

Produced for Focus Readers by Red Line Editorial.

Content Consultant: Melodie Andrews, PhD, Associate Professor of History, Minnesota State University, Mankato

Photographs ©: Victorian Traditions/Shutterstock Images, cover, 1; North Wind Picture Archives, 4–5, 10–11, 13, 15, 17, 18–19, 20, 23, 24–25, 27; Sarony & Major/Library of Congress, 7; switchpipipi/iStockphoto, 29

ISBN
978-1-63517-249-2 (hardcover)
978-1-63517-314-7 (paperback)
978-1-63517-444-1 (ebook pdf)
978-1-63517-379-6 (hosted ebook)

Library of Congress Control Number: 2017935901

Printed in the United States of America
Mankato, MN
June, 2017

ABOUT THE AUTHOR

Wil Mara is the author of more than 200 books, many of which are educational titles for children. His interest in American history goes back to his childhood, spurred in part by a trip to Washington, DC, in the late 1970s during which he met President Jimmy Carter.

TABLE OF CONTENTS

CHAPTER 1

ANGER IN THE COLONIES

In the early 1770s, many American colonists were growing angry. They disliked the way the British government was **taxing** them. The government needed this money to pay debts. However, the taxes had been created without approval from the colonists.

Great Britain taxed the colonists to help pay for the French and Indian War (1754–1763).

The government believed it had the right to make decisions about colonists' taxes.

Some of the colonists started to take action. In December 1773, a group boarded three ships in Boston Harbor. A large shipment of British tea was aboard. The colonists dumped the tea into the water. This event became known as the Boston Tea Party. It was a response to Great Britain's tax on tea.

The British government sent soldiers to the colonies. A few fights broke out. People were killed on both sides.

In the fall of 1774, the colonists held a meeting. They wanted to decide how to respond to the British government.

Colonists knew the Boston Tea Party was illegal, so some disguised themselves as American Indians.

The meeting was known as the Continental Congress. Many people at the meeting hoped to fix the relationship with the government.

By the spring of 1775, the colonists were at war with Great Britain. The Second Continental Congress met in the summer. Many people at the meeting still wanted to remain with Great Britain.

However, others believed the time had come to break away.

Even after the war started, most colonists were not sure whether they wanted **independence**. That started to change in January 1776. Thomas Paine wrote a pamphlet called *Common Sense*. It made strong arguments about why independence was needed. The pamphlet became very popular.

People's opinions slowly started to change. More and more colonists believed the government was not respecting their rights. The government had refused to get their approval on taxes. British soldiers had killed a number of colonists.

And *Common Sense* had reached a wide audience. With these things in mind, the Continental Congress made a difficult decision. The colonies had to declare their independence.

EVENTS LEADING UP TO THE DECLARATION

1750

1754–1763
The French and Indian War

1764
The Sugar Act, The Currency Act

1765
The Stamp Act, The Quartering Act

1767
The Townshend Revenue Act

1770
The Boston Massacre

1773
The Tea Act, The Boston Tea Party

1774
The "Intolerable Acts," First Continental Congress

1775
Battles of Lexington and Concord, Second Continental Congress

1776
Publication of *Common Sense*

1780

CHAPTER 2

SEEKING INDEPENDENCE

In the spring of 1776, some colonies started declaring their independence from Great Britain. Rhode Island was the first. On May 4, the colony passed a **resolution**. It stated that Rhode Island was free of British rule. Other colonies soon did the same.

The war had been going on for more than a year when colonies began declaring independence.

The Second Continental Congress held a meeting. The members agreed they needed a declaration covering all 13 colonies. On May 15, they passed a **preamble**. It said the colonies planned to break away from Great Britain. However, a more detailed document was necessary. Congress wanted to make sure their reasons for seeking independence were clear.

In early June, the Second Continental Congress selected five of its members to create the declaration. They were Thomas Jefferson, Benjamin Franklin, John Adams, Robert Livingston, and Robert Sherman. The five men discussed

Members of the Second Continental Congress discuss Jefferson's first draft.

the basic ideas that should be included. They also decided Jefferson would write the document. Jefferson was known to be good with words.

Jefferson finished the first **draft** in less than three weeks. After that, the other four members gave him suggestions.

They told him what he should change. When Jefferson made the changes, he showed the document to the full Congress. The members agreed on a few more changes. Finally, the Declaration of Independence was ready. It stated that the British government was harming the people it was supposed to protect. The document then listed the colonists' many complaints against the government. It also said all men had certain rights.

The Congress voted for independence on July 2. John Adams believed this date would become a holiday for the new country. However, a few more changes were made to the Declaration. So, the

The Second Continental Congress gathers to sign the Declaration of Independence.

final wording was not approved until July 4. On that day, printers began making copies of the Declaration. They sent it out to the colonists. Before long, celebrations took place around the country. Meanwhile, fighting in the war continued.

JEFFERSON AND SLAVERY

Thomas Jefferson's first draft stirred much debate. One passage mentioned slavery. Jefferson himself was a slaveholder. But he was opposed to the idea of slavery. Slaveholders have "waged cruel war against human nature itself," he wrote. Jefferson said slavery went against the "most sacred rights of life and liberty." He was saying all people have a right to be free. Even so, he freed only two of his slaves during his lifetime.

Jefferson also said slaveholders were "exciting those very people to rise in arms among us." He was warning that enslaved people might grow angry. And someday, they might rise up and fight.

In the end, most of Jefferson's text about slavery was removed from the Declaration of Independence. Many members of the Continental

Millions of enslaved black people were forced to work on farms.

Congress were slaveholders. They made a great deal of money from slavery. For this reason, they did not want slavery to end.

UNITED WE

CHAPTER 3

THE REACTION

Copies of the Declaration were sent out across the country. Some copies were put on ships so they could go to other countries. In America, copies were read aloud in public places. Teachers talked about it to their students. Many parents talked about it to their children.

A crowd gathers to hear a reading of the Declaration of Independence.

Supporters of American independence force a Loyalist to leave.

But not all colonists liked the idea of independence. Many of them remained loyal to the British government.

These people were known as Loyalists. They continued to hope the relationship between the two sides could be fixed. The Declaration of Independence made Loyalists more worried than ever. As a result, some made the difficult decision to leave America.

A few Loyalists sailed back to Great Britain. Some went to the other countries under British control. One of the most common destinations was the British colonies in Canada. Many of the Loyalists who went to Canada were rewarded for their loyalty. The British often gave them money. Other times they promised land.

Some Loyalists in the southern colonies thought the journey to Canada was too far. They decided to go south instead. Florida and Jamaica were common spots.

News of the Declaration arrived in Great Britain in August 1776. The Declaration was soon printed in several British newspapers. Many people read it. The British people waited to hear what King George III would say. He finally spoke to the British government in October. He said the colonists were acting illegally. Great Britain was not willing to give them independence. Instead, the king promised that Great Britain would continue fighting the war.

George III was the king of Great Britain from 1760 to 1820.

CHAPTER 4

INDEPENDENCE BECOMES REALITY

Great Britain's leaders were very confident they would win the war. Their soldiers were well trained. And they had hired German troops to help fight the colonists. But the Continental Army, led by George Washington, refused to give up. The colonists also got help from other countries.

George Washington leads the Continental Army to a winter camp in late 1777.

For instance, France helped the Continental Army win some of its most important victories. France had endured years of fighting with Great Britain. So, the country's leaders agreed to help the colonists.

As the years went on, the war began to lose support in Great Britain. The British had suffered too many **casualties**. They had also lost territory and spent a great deal of money. Many British people demanded that the fighting come to an end.

The British finally surrendered to colonial forces in 1781. This put an end to the fighting. In 1783, a peace treaty

Benjamin Franklin (right) discusses the peace treaty with a British negotiator.

officially ended the war. It also made the Declaration of Independence a reality. The United States was free of British rule.

The Declaration of Independence was based on a simple idea. A government should have the **consent** of its people.

If a government fails to do so, the Declaration says, “it is the right of the people to alter or to **abolish** it.”

The document lists many of King George’s worst actions against the colonies. One example says, “He has dissolved **Representative** Houses repeatedly.” The colonists wanted to keep their own governments. This was one of the many reasons they decided to break away from Great Britain.

In the years since the Declaration was written, it has inspired many nations around the world. More than 100 countries have drafted their own declarations of independence. And many of them borrowed language directly from the American document. To this day, the Declaration of Independence remains a powerful statement of human rights.

TAKING INSPIRATION

These are some of the countries that have made their own declarations with wording inspired by the US Declaration of Independence.

FOCUS ON

THE DECLARATION OF INDEPENDENCE

Write your answers on a separate piece of paper.

1. Write a letter to a friend explaining the main ideas of Chapter 1.

2. Do you think King George was right to continue the war after he read the Declaration? Why or why not?

3. Who wrote the first draft of the Declaration of Independence?

- **A.** Benjamin Franklin
- **B.** Thomas Jefferson
- **C.** John Adams

4. Why did many Loyalists move to Canada?

- **A.** They wanted to live in a place that was under British control.
- **B.** They wanted to write their own Declaration of Independence.
- **C.** They wanted to gather supplies for the war against the colonists.

Answer key on page 32.

GLOSSARY

abolish
To officially end something.

casualties
People who are injured or killed in a war.

consent
Permission for something to happen.

draft
A version of a document that is likely to change.

independence
The ability to make decisions without being controlled by another government.

preamble
An introduction or statement of intent to do something.

representative
Made up of people who speak on behalf of a larger group.

resolution
A promise to take a certain action.

taxing
Adding money to the cost of a purchase and giving it to the government.

TO LEARN MORE

BOOKS

Meinking, Mary. *The Declaration of Independence*. Mankato, MN: The Child's World, 2016.

Miller, Mirella S. *12 Questions about the Declaration of Independence*. Mankato, MN: 12-Story Library, 2016.

Morey, Allan. *A Timeline History of the Declaration of Independence*. Minneapolis: Lerner Publications, 2015.

NOTE TO EDUCATORS

Visit **www.focusreaders.com** to find lesson plans, activities, links, and other resources related to this title.

INDEX

Answer Key: 1. Answers will vary; **2.** Answers will vary; **3.** B; **4.** A